D1311709

Math Made Easy

Extra MATH Practice

Grade **3**

Math Workbook

Author Sean McArdle
Consultant Alison Tribley

LONDON, NEW YORK, MUNICH, MELBOURNE, AND DELHI

DK UK
Senior Editor Deborah Lock
Art Director Martin Wilson
Publishing Director Sophie Mitchell
Pre-production Francesca Wardell
Jacket Designer Martin Wilson
US Editor Nancy Ellwood
Math Consultant Alison Tribley

DK Delhi
Editorial Monica Saigal, Tanya Desai
Design Pallavi Narain, Dheeraj Arora,
Tanvi Nathyal, Jyotsna Khosla
DTP Designer Anita Yadav

First American Edition, 2013
Published in the United States by DK Publishing
375 Hudson Street, New York, New York 10014

13 14 15 16 17 10 9 8 7 6 5 4 3 2 1
001-187398-July/2013

Published in Great Britain by Dorling Kindersley Limited.

DK books are available at special discounts when
purchased in bulk for sales promotions, premiums,
fund-raising, or educational use.
For details, contact: DK Publishing Special Markets
375 Hudson Street, New York, New York 10014
SpecialSales@dk.com

A catalog record for this book
is available from the Library of Congress
ISBN: 978-1-4654-0935-5
Printed and bound in China by L. Rex Printing Co., Ltd.

All images © Dorling Kindersley.
For further information see: www.dkimages.com

Discover more at
www.dk.com

Contents

This chart lists all the topics in the book. Once you have completed each page, stick a star in the correct box below.

Page	Topic	Star
4	Place value	☆
5	Negative numbers	☆
6	Count forward and backward	☆
7	Ordering numbers	☆
8	Rounding	☆
9	Comparing numbers	☆
10	Fractions of numbers	☆
11	Fractions of shapes	☆
12	Quarters	☆
13	Calculator	☆

Circle the "tens" digit in each number.

④5   12,458   7,219   9,567   700

Circle the "hundreds" digit in each number.

184   365   12,456   5,786   9,200

Circle the "thousands" digit in each number.

5,000   2,163   11,546   5,284   9,534

654 can be written as 600 + 50 + 4. This is called the **expanded form**. Write each number in its expanded form.

423 _____   9,406 _____

710 _____   8,056 _____

612 _____   1,428 _____

649 _____   10,417 _____

8,000 + 700 + 60 + 9 can be written as 8,769. This is called the **standard form**. Write each number in its standard form.

2,000 + 400 + 7 _____   4,000 + 200 + 30 + 5 _____

6,000 + 50 + 8 _____   9,000 + 4 _____

Look at this number line.

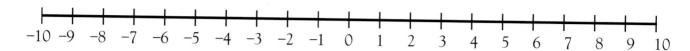

Add 1 to each number. **Note**: When you add, you move to the right on the number line.

3   4   7   9   1   0   − 2

− 10   8   4   6   − 3   − 9

Subtract 1 from each number. **Note**: When you subtract, you move left on the number line.

8   5   10   1   − 3   − 9

2   9   −5   4   − 8   − 7

Add 3 to each number. **Hint**: Move to the right.

4   7   0   − 7   − 5

5   − 3   − 9   6   − 10

Subtract 4 from each number. **Hint**: Move to the left.

4   − 5   9   10   − 4

5   2   3   − 1   − 6

What is 3 more than these numbers?

7 [10]   28 [ ]   99 [ ]   80 [ ]   107 [ ]

What is 3 less than these numbers?

11 [ ]   70 [ ]   92 [ ]   48 [ ]   101 [ ]

What is 4 more than these numbers?

6 [ ]   17 [ ]   59 [ ]   31 [ ]   98 [ ]

What is 4 less than these numbers?

11 [ ]   34 [ ]   43 [ ]   98 [ ]   102 [ ]

Fill in the missing numbers.

92   95   98   101

109   106   103

88   92   96

113   109   105

Put each row of numbers in order, starting with the smallest.

213	312	123	230	32
32				

841	148	184	481	814

Put each row of numbers in order, starting with the largest.

672	276	627	267	726

1,500	1,005	1,050	5,000	5,100

Put this row in order, starting with the smallest amount.

$2.60	$6.20	$2.06	$6.02	$0.26

Put this row in order, starting with the largest amount.

$12.34	$21.43	$43.21	$43.12	$34.21

For each sum, put these numbers in order, starting with the largest. Then add.

50 + 200 + 8 = 200 + 50 + 8 = 258

7 + 60 + 400 = ___ + ___ + ___ = ___

12 + 750 = ___ + ___ = ___

24 + 370 = ___ + ___ = ___

Round each number to the nearest 10.

14 10   9   55   26

11   38   99   72

883   451   724   906

107   2,345   4,189   6,503

Round each number to the nearest 100.

263   485   210   895

481   673   950   420

762   380   266   750

Round each number to the nearest 1,000.

1,070   1,430   3,760   2,888

4,500   6,731   9,244   6,499

8,050   6,370   7,500   9,482

Circle the smaller number.

(3 x 4)   or   7 + 6   7 + 8   or   20 – 4   2 x 8   or   3 x 5

10 x 3   or   18 + 13   5 x 4   or   10 + 9   15 – 3   or   8 + 6

Circle the larger number.

10 x 4   or   19 + 13   8 + 9   or   3 x 6   12 + 12   or   7 x 3

5 x 3   or   8 + 6   10 + 12   or   5 x 5   7 + 13   or   30 – 9

Circle the smaller amount.

$2.00   or   80 ¢ + 70 ¢   65 ¢ – 25 ¢ or 56 ¢ – 30 ¢

$1.00   or   70 ¢ + 35 ¢   90 ¢ – 25 ¢ or 65 ¢ – 10 ¢

Circle the larger amount.

$5 + $2   or   250 ¢ + 250 ¢   47 ¢ – 8 ¢   or   35 ¢ + 3¢

$2.50   or $3.00 – 40 ¢   60 ¢ – 15 ¢ or 70 ¢ – 20 ¢

Circle the amount that is between $3.00 and $4.00.

$2.30 + 65 ¢ $5.00 – $1.50 $5.00 – 35 ¢

Circle the amount that is between 2 ft and 3 ft.

1.5 ft + 2.5 ft   6.5 ft – 2.5 ft   4 ft – 1.5 ft

Circle half ($\frac{1}{2}$) of the vegetables in each group.

Circle a quarter ($\frac{1}{4}$) of the fruit in each row.

What is half ($\frac{1}{2}$) of each number?

6 ____   12 ____   10 ____   20 ____   4 ____

What is a quarter ($\frac{1}{4}$) of each number?

4 ____   8 ____   16 ____   20 ____   12 ____

Half of a number is 3. What is the number?   ____

Half of a number is 6. What is the number?   ____

A quarter of a number is 1. What is the number?   ____

A quarter of a number is 5. What is the number?   ____

Shade $\frac{1}{2}$ of each shape.

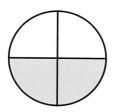 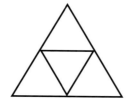 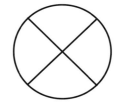

Now shade $\frac{1}{2}$ of the same shapes in a different way.

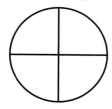 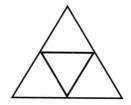 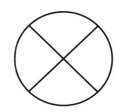

Shade $\frac{2}{3}$ of each shape.

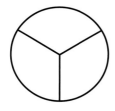 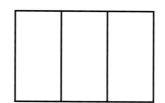 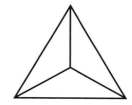

Shade $\frac{3}{5}$ of each shape.

  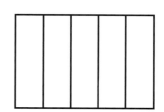

Shade $\frac{7}{10}$ of each shape.

 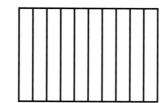 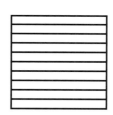

What is a quarter ($\frac{1}{4}$) of each number?

12 [3]   16 [ ]   40 [ ]   28 [ ]

What is a quarter ($\frac{1}{4}$) of each amount?

4 ¢ [ ]   20 ¢ [ ]   12 ¢ [ ]   16 ¢ [ ]

How much is a quarter ($\frac{1}{4}$) of 40 ¢?

[ ]

Fido eats 8 biscuits each day. Fido has a quarter ($\frac{1}{4}$) of the biscuits for breakfast. How many biscuits does Fido have for breakfast? [ ]

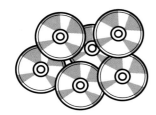 Daisy is given 20 CDs by her sister. Daisy gives a quarter ($\frac{1}{4}$) of the CDs to her brother. How many CDs does Daisy give to her brother?

[ ]

Shen has to work for one hour but stops after a quarter of an hour. How long is a quarter of an hour in minutes? [ ]

Darius has to wait 24 minutes for a bus. He has waited a quarter ($\frac{1}{4}$) of that time. How long does Darius still have to wait?

[ ]

Use a calculator to work out these problems.

7 x 12 = 84   9 x 9 =   10 x 12 =

7 x 6 =   14 x 10 =   12 x 50 =

16 x 3 =   200 x 6 =   120 x 7 =

12 x 8 =   20 x 20 =   150 x 6 =

26 + 49 + 58 =   74 + 59 + 82 =   29 + 69 + 84 =

546 + 512 =   785 + 897 =   209 + 109 + 56 =

432 + 777 =   812 + 564 =   231 + 321 + 412 =

576 − 299 =   600 − 345 =   708 − 544 =

1,000 − 564 =   1,645 − 789 =   1,705 − 805 =

5,634 − 4,867 =   4,554 − 3,667 =   9,045 − 9,044 =

86 ÷ 2 =   100 ÷ 25 =   40 ÷ 8 =

160 ÷ 8 =   240 ÷ 12 =   300 ÷ 15 =

4,800 ÷ 200 =   5,000 ÷ 25 =   196 ÷ 14 =

Jake has to share $280 equally between himself and his four sisters.

How much will they each receive?

Which child has the most money?

Nada	Barbara	Ann	Harris
$2,304	$432	$4,023	$3,402

....

This thermometer shows the temperature. Overnight, the temperature drops by 14°. What is the temperature at night?

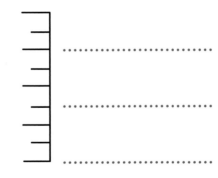

Write the children's names in order of height, starting with the shortest.

....

....

Harris	Doris	Dave	Taylor
3.45 ft	4.90 ft	3.20 ft	4.10 ft

....

Round each amount to the nearest dollar.

85 ¢ $1.30 $3.65 $2.50 $9.45

James thinks of a number and then multiplies it by 3.
James then adds on 5 and gets the number 17.

What number did James begin with?

Maggie has $24 and spends one-quarter at a clothes shop.

How much will Maggie have left?

Molly is going on vacation and can only pack half her shirts.
Cross out half of the shirts.

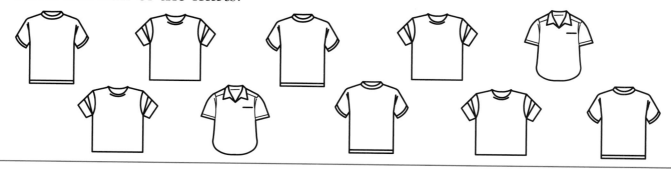

Peter has $5.00 and gives one-tenth ($\frac{1}{10}$) away to charity.

How much does he give to charity?

What fraction of $1.00 is 25 ¢?

Use a calculator to help you.

45 + 24 − 16 =

30 + 40 + 50 + 60 + 70 + 80 =

4,231 − 1,967 =

120 + 89 − 53 =

Write the answers.

$9 + 8 + 7 = \boxed{24}$ $10 + 8 + 7 = \boxed{}$ $20 + 17 + 14 = \boxed{}$

$11 + 5 + 3 = \boxed{}$ $15 + 10 + 5 = \boxed{}$ $30 + 20 + 10 = \boxed{}$

$50 + 30 + 10 = \boxed{}$ $12 + 11 + 10 = \boxed{}$ $21 + 11 + 1 = \boxed{}$

$7 + 14 + 21 = \boxed{}$ $9 + 18 + 30 = \boxed{}$ $50 + 30 + 20 = \boxed{}$

$40 + 18 + 20 = \boxed{}$ $30 + 19 + 10 = \boxed{}$ $10 + 23 + 40 = \boxed{}$

$70 + 9 + 10 = \boxed{}$ $50 + 17 + 20 = \boxed{}$ $40 + 20 + 40 = \boxed{}$

$17 + 18 + 19 = \boxed{}$ $23 + 24 + 25 = \boxed{}$ $36 + 37 + 38 = \boxed{}$

$51 + 52 + 53 = \boxed{}$ $35 + 45 + 55 = \boxed{}$ $20 + 80 + 60 = \boxed{}$

Write the answers.

23	45	19	56	38	73
34	16	15	42	13	12
+ 42	+ 18	+ 32	+ 17	+ 25	+ 15
99					

Write the answers.

$20 - 7 =$ 13 $34 - 18 =$ $42 - 19 =$ $23 - 22 =$

$50 - 27 =$ $44 - 35 =$ $21 - 19 =$ $50 - 36 =$

$53 - 26 =$ $71 - 68 =$ $49 - 17 =$ $60 - 12 =$

$50 - 19 =$ $40 - 18 =$ $30 - 17 =$ $20 - 16 =$

$100 - 40 =$ $100 - 65 =$ $100 - 32 =$ $100 - 17 =$

$100 - 45 =$ $100 - 70 =$ $100 - 23 =$ $100 - 71 =$

Write the answers.

43	67	80	120	105	102
− 21	− 14	− 54	− 30	− 45	− 56
22					

Matilda owns 145 pairs of shoes but gives 62 pairs away to a charity shop.

How many pairs of shoes does Matilda have left?

Write the answers.

3 sets of 2 = 6

3 x 2 = 6

4 sets of 2 = ☐

☐ x ☐ = ☐

2 sets of 2 = ☐

☐ x ☐ = ☐

2 sets of 5 = ☐

☐ x ☐ = ☐

Write the answers.

1 x 2 = ☐   2 x 2 = ☐   3 x 2 = ☐   4 x 2 = ☐

5 x 2 = ☐   6 x 2 = ☐   9 x 2 = ☐   10 x 2 = ☐

2 x 3 = ☐   2 x 4 = ☐   2 x 6 = ☐   2 x 8 = ☐

2 x 1 = ☐   2 x 3 = ☐   2 x 5 = ☐   2 x 7 = ☐

What number is missing?

☐ x 3 = 6   ☐ x 5 = 10   ☐ x 8 = 16   ☐ x 7 = 14

☐ x 4 = 8   ☐ x 10 = 20   ☐ x 6 = 12   ☐ x 9 = 18

What are 2 groups of each amount?

5 ¢ [10 ¢]   10 ¢ [   ]   20 ¢ [   ]   50 ¢ [   ] $2 [   ]

Multiply each amount by 2.

8 ¢ [   ]   12 ¢ [   ]   25 ¢ [   ]   30 ¢ [   ]   40 ¢ [   ]

Write the answers.

2 x 8 = [   ]   2 x 10 = [   ]   2 x 11 = [   ]   2 x 6 = [   ]

7 x 2 = [   ]   12 x 2 = [   ]   10 x 2 = [   ]   2 x 9 = [   ]

What is the missing number?

10 x [ ] = 20   8 x [ ] = 16   5 x [ ] = 10   6 x [ ] = 12

[ ] x 7 = 14   2 x [ ] = 22   [ ] x 9 = 18   2 x [ ] = 100

20 x [ ] = 40   30 x [ ] = 60   40 x [ ] = 80   2 x [ ] = 50

100 x 2 = [   ]   200 x 2 = [   ]   300 x 2 = [   ]   400 x 2 = [   ]

Try this:

Start with 2, then double it, then double that
number, and then double that number.

What number do you have?   [   ]

Match each dog to the right bone with a line.

Complete the sum.

1 x 10 = ___   10 x 4 in. = ___   4 x 10 = ___   50 x 10 = ___

2 x 10 = ___   10 x 8 in. = ___   6 x 10 = ___   11 x 10 = ___

20 x 10 = ___   10 x 12 ¢ = ___   40 x 10 = ___   30 x 10 = ___

8 x 10 = ___   10 x 6 ¢ = ___   7 x 10 = ___   9 x 10 = ___

___ x 10 = 30   ___ x 9 = 90   ___ x 10 = 0   ___ x 10 = 70

5 ¢ x ___ = 50 ¢   3 ¢ x ___ = 30 ¢   20 ¢ x ___ = 200 ¢

How many tens are the same as 80? ___

How many tens are the same as 100? ___

How many tens are the same as 200? ___

Match each mouse to the right cheese with a line.

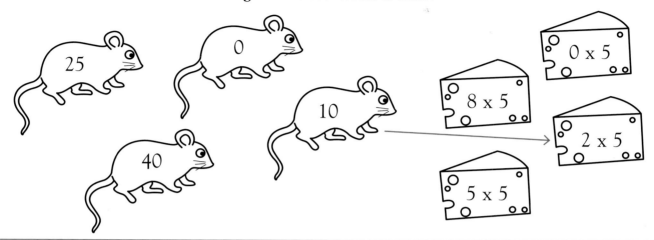

Write the answers.

4 x 5 = [ ]   8 x 5 = [ ]   5 x 3 ¢ = [ ]   5 x 0 = [ ]

1 x 5 = [ ]   11 x 5 = [ ]   5 x 9 ¢ = [ ]   5 x 12 ¢ = [ ]

6 x 5 = [ ]   7 x 5 = [ ]   5 x 10 in. = [ ]   5 x [ ] = 30

12 x 5 = [ ]   0 x 5 = [ ]   5 x 6 ¢ = [ ]   5 x [ ] = 45

Circle the numbers that are **not** multiples of 5.

5   10   13   40   90   55   120   18   22   47   100

Write the answers.

5 + 5 = [ ]   2 groups of 5 = [ ]   5 groups of 2 are [ ]

5 x 2 = [ ]   3 groups of 5 = [ ]   3 groups of 5 are [ ]

Complete the grids.

X	2	6	8	11	9
2	4				
5	10				

X	0	1	8	6	4
2					
5					
10					

X	2	5	6	7	10	11	12
2							
5							
10							

X	3		8		
2		12		14	22
5		30		35	55
10		60		70	110

Write the answers.

9 x 3 = 27   10 x 6 = ___   8 x 4 = ___   6 x 11 = ___

7 x 5 = ___   9 x 4 = ___   6 x 5 = ___   10 x 10 = ___

12 x 2 = ___   12 x 4 = ___   12 x 10 = ___   12 x 0 = ___

4 x 7 = ___   5 x 9 = ___   3 x 8 = ___   7 x 10 = ___

1 x 1 = ___   3 x 3 = ___   5 x 5 = ___   6 x 6 = ___

7 x 7 = ___   8 x 8 = ___   9 x 9 = ___   0 x 0 = ___

Write the answers.

| 8 | 7 | 9 | 10 |
x 4	x 6	x 5	x 8

| 12 | 13 | 14 | 15 |
x 7	x 4	x 6	x 8

Don collects 12 new sports cards
every day for a week.

How many cards will Don
have at the end of the week?

Circle the numbers that are multiples of 3.

(12)   14   16   18   20   22   24   26   28   30

Circle the numbers that are multiples of 4.

2   4   6   8   10   12   14   16   18   20

Circle the numbers that are multiples of 5.

2   7   10   14   19   20   25   28   33   42

Circle the numbers that are multiples of 6.

4   6   8   10   12   14   16   18   20   24

Circle the numbers that are multiples of 10.

5   10   20   30   55   75   90   95   100   200

What is the smallest number that is a multiple of 3 and 4?

What is the smallest number that is a multiple of 2 and 5?

What is the smallest number that is a multiple of 3 and 5?

What is the smallest number that is a multiple of 2 and 4?

What is the smallest number that is a multiple of 3 and 10?

Write the answers.

20 ÷ 4 = 5   20 ÷ 2 =   20 ÷ 5 =

20 ÷ 10 =   12 ÷ 2 =   12 ÷ 6 =

12 ÷ 3 =   12 ÷ 4 =   18 ÷ 3 =

18 ÷ 6 =   18 ÷ 9 =   18 ÷ 2 =

30 ÷ 6 =   24 ÷ 2 =   40 ÷ 10 =

28 ÷ 7 =   44 ÷ 4 =   25 ÷ 5 =

32 ÷ 8 =   24 ÷ 6 =   12 ÷ 12 =

14 ÷ 2 =   32 ÷ 4 =   56 ÷ 7 =

10 ÷ 5 =   14 ÷ 2 =   20 ÷ 4 =

24 ÷ 3 =   12 ÷ 2 =   15 ÷ 5 =

21 ÷ 3 =   27 ÷ 3 =   16 ÷ 4 =

36 ÷ 4 =   28 ÷ 4 =   30 ÷ 5 =

50 ÷ 10 =   70 ÷ 10 =   60 ÷ 10 =

40 ÷ 10 =   16 ÷ 2 =   22 ÷ 2 =

4 ÷ 2 =   14 ÷ 2 =   24 ÷ 3 =

45 ÷ 5 =   44 ÷ 4 =   12 ÷ 6 =

I add 16 to a number and then have 40.
What number did I begin with?

24

I subtract 25 from a number and have 14 left.
What number did I start with?

I multiplied a number by 6 and now have 54.
What number did I begin with?

Danny has a collection of 28 comics and
buys another 14. How many comics does
Danny have now?

I divided a number by 8 and now have 2.
What number did I begin with?

After adding 20 ¢ to some money, Gill has 75 ¢.
How much did Gill have to start with?

Margaret has to share 100 grapes between herself
and her three sisters. How many grapes do they each
receive? **Hint:** Margaret wants some grapes too.

Peter adds three numbers together. Two of the numbers
are 8 and 7 and the total is 20. What number is missing?

Justin knows that six times a number is 48 but has
forgotten the number! Remind Justin what the number is.

Jonas has lost some money. He started
with $1.00 but now has only 58 ¢. How
much has Jonas lost?

Fatima has this money but needs $2.00

How much more does Fatima need?

70 ¢

Angelo gives $3.50 to his sister and $1.50 to a friend.

How much has Angelo given away?

Chantal receives $1.30 change after giving
the storekeeper $5.

How much did Chantal spend?

 Otto buys a Chubby burger for $2.55 and pays
with three $1 bills.

How much change will Otto receive?

Sasha is given money by her
relatives on her birthday.

How much does Sasha
receive in total?

 $10 $10 $5

From Mom   From Dad   From Granny

Rudo wants to buy a toy that costs $8.60.
Rudo has $5.30.

How much more does Rudo need to buy the toy?

When Henry's dad empties his pockets, he finds he has one $10 bill, two $5 bills, four 25 ¢ coins, and five 10 ¢ coins.

How much money has Henry's dad found?

Henry's mom finds this money behind some cushions—four $1 bills, five 25 ¢ coins, two 10 ¢ coins, and seven 1 ¢ coins.

How much money has Henry's mom found?

Henry's mom and dad put their money together.

How much do they have in total?

Jack and Jane together have $25. They spend their money on a take out meal that costs $30.

How much more do they need?

What amount is missing?

$5   + $5   + $10   + $20   +   _____   = $50

Write the answer.

How many 5 ¢ coins are the same as $1.00?

How many 10 ¢ coins are the same as $1.80?

How many 25 ¢ coins are the same as $2.00?

Write each amount in two ways.

Example: Thirty-five cents is either 35 ¢ or $0.35

Seven cents ⬜ ⬜   Ninety cents ⬜ ⬜

Twenty-nine cents ⬜ ⬜   Forty-two cents ⬜ ⬜

Thirty-one cents ⬜ ⬜   Fifteen cents ⬜ ⬜

Sixty-seven cents ⬜ ⬜   Fifty-five cents ⬜ ⬜

Ninety-three cents ⬜ ⬜   Seventy-eight cents ⬜ ⬜

Write the answers.

$1.20 + $0.80 = $2 $1.30 + $1.60 = ⬜ $2.10 + $1.70 = ⬜

$1.30 + $0.50 = ⬜ $5.00 − $2.50 = ⬜ $1.45 + $0.65 = ⬜

$2.50 + $1.50 = ⬜ $1.40 + $2.30 = ⬜ $5.25 + $1.15 = ⬜

$1.35 + $1.45 = ⬜ $0.60 + $0.85 = ⬜ $1.60 + $1.60 = ⬜

$4.45 + $0.70 = ⬜ $2.05 + $1.75 = ⬜ $1.00 − $0.73 = ⬜

$1.00 − $0.30 = ⬜ $5.90 + $0.20 = ⬜ $2.00 − $1.50 = ⬜

$2.00 − $0.50 = ⬜ $5.00 − $3.00 = ⬜ $10.00 − $7.50 = ⬜

Write the answers.

What is $1.60 plus 45 ¢? ⬜   How much is $5.00 minus 8 ¢? ⬜

What is $3.80 plus 70 ¢? ⬜   How much is $2.00 minus 30 ¢? ⬜

Complete this grid.

X	4		10	
5	20	45	50	
2		18		12

Write the answers.

24	38	40	51
− 17	− 12	− 23	− 36

Bart has to mark these products for Homer.
Help Bart to mark the products right (✔) or wrong (✗).

8 x 3 = 42   5 x 6 = 30   2 x 12 = 22

10 x 5 = 50   3 x 9 = 24   8 x 4 = 31

What is the smallest number that is a multiple
of 4 and 5?

What is the largest number that is a multiple
of 3 and 2 but less than 20?

Lucy has to share 3 pizzas equally
between herself and three friends.
Each pizza has 8 pieces.

How many pieces of pizza will each girl receive?

Share 20 apples equally among 4 children.

How many apples will each child get?

Write the answers.

12 shared by 2 =

12 shared by 3 =

12 shared by 4 =

12 shared by 12 =

Write the missing numbers.

8 + ☐ = 15

5 x ☐ = 15

30 ÷ ☐ = 15

21 − ☐ = 15

Stefan is given 20 ¢ and now has 75 ¢.
How much did Stefan have before?

Anzelm has 45 model animals and buys another 18.
How many model animals does Anzelm have now?

Add each list.

$3.20	$1.80	$2.60
$1.40	$1.30	$1.20
+ $5.00	+ $1.60	+ $2.80

This is a ruler.

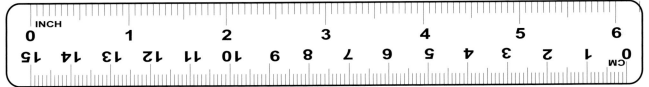

What length is shown on each ruler?

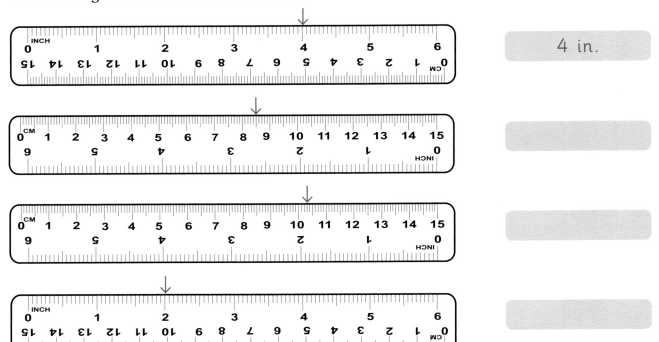

4 in.

Mark the lengths on the ruler.

3.7 cm

10.3 cm

$3\frac{1}{2}$ in.

$5\frac{1}{2}$ in.

This is a part of a measuring tape.

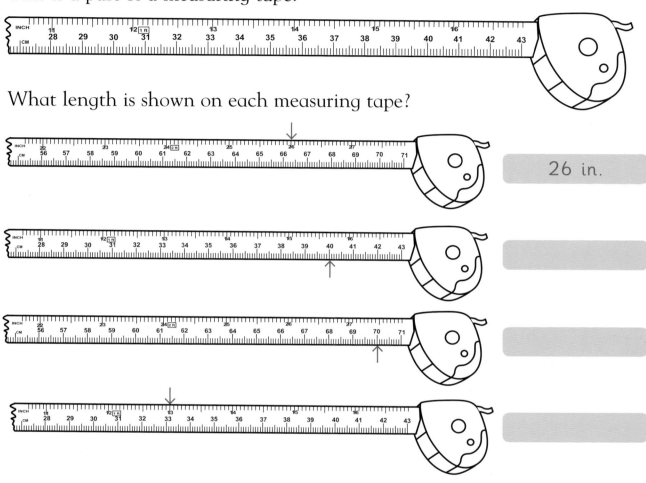

What length is shown on each measuring tape?

26 in.

Mark the lengths on the tape.

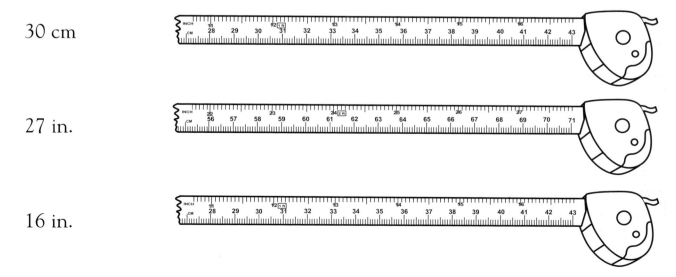

30 cm

27 in.

16 in.

Show the time on each clock.

2:10

5:40

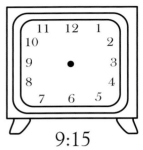
9:15

7:50

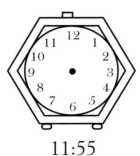
11:55

10:20

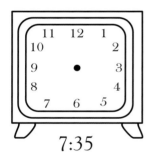
7:35

1:05

8:05

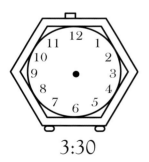
3:30

5:05

6:25

Write the answers.

What is the time 10 minutes after 8:30?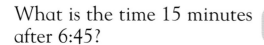

What is the time 20 minutes before 9:00?

What is the time 15 minutes after 6:45?

What is the time 20 minutes before 5:30?

What is the time on each clock face?

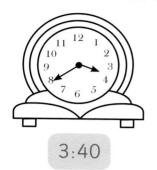   

3:40

Write these times on the clock faces.

6:20   5:40

7:55

4:35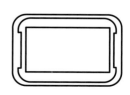

Look at the drawing and answer the questions.

The girl makes a quarter turn to her right. What animal does she see?

Dog

The girl is facing the dog and makes a half-turn. What animal does she see?

The girl is facing the horse and makes a quarter turn to her left. What animal does she see?

The girl faces the cow and makes a clockwise three-quarter turn. What animal is she facing?

The girl faces the monkey and makes a full turn clockwise. What animal does she see?

Look at the spinner and answer the questions.

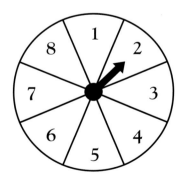

If the arrow spins a quarter turn clockwise, which number will it be on?

If the arrow spins a quarter turn counterclockwise, which number will it be on?

If the arrow spins around to number 6, how much has it turned?

Amy asked children in her school about favorite places to go on vacation. Amy recorded her information on a tally chart.

Favorite Cities

Cities	Number of Votes
Boston	ЦЦ ЦЦ ЦЦ ЦЦ ЦЦ |||
New York City	ЦЦ ЦЦ ЦЦ ЦЦ ЦЦ ЦЦ ЦЦ ЦЦ	
Washington, DC	ЦЦ ЦЦ ЦЦ ||
San Francisco	ЦЦ ЦЦ ||||
Honolulu	ЦЦ ЦЦ ЦЦ ЦЦ ||

Amy forgot to record 4 votes for New York City. Add these to the chart.

Which was the most popular choice?

How many children liked this city?

Which was the least popular city?

How many children liked this city?

How many more children preferred Boston to Washington, DC?

How many children did Amy ask in total?

Which city had 17 votes?

How many votes did Honolulu and San Francisco have in total?

Put the cities in order of votes, with the least popular first.

Graphs

Mike asks his class about their favorite cities visited during the summer vacations. He records his findings on a bar graph.

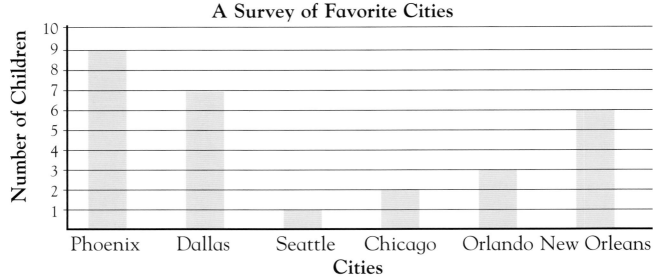

A Survey of Favorite Cities

Rank the cities in order of popularity, starting with the least favorite.

....

How many children preferred Phoenix?

Which two cities had a total of 13?

....

The pictograph shows how many children took part in various sports.

A Survey of Favorite Sports

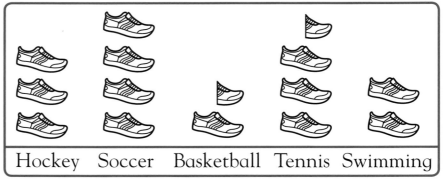

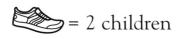 = 2 children

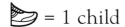 = 1 child

Which is the most popular sport?

....

Which sport had 7 votes?

....

How many children liked basketball?

How many children took part in the survey?

Give the correct name for each shape.

Oval

....

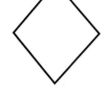

....

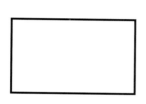
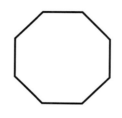
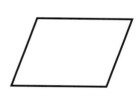

....

Look at the shapes above. List the shapes that have curved sides.

....

Look at the shapes above. List the shapes that have right angles.

....

Draw a pentagon that is not regular. | Draw a right-angle triangle.

Is the dotted line a line of symmetry?

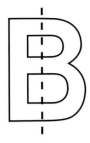

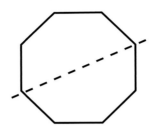

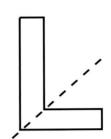

No
....

....

....

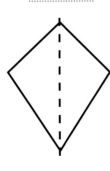

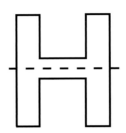

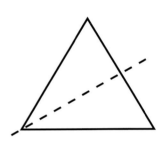

....

....

....

Complete each drawing.

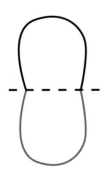

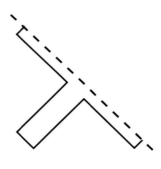

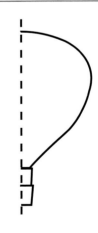

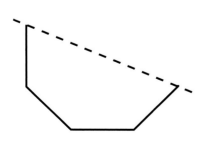

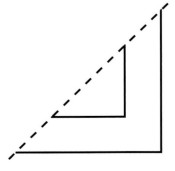

Look carefully for the right angles and mark them on the shapes.

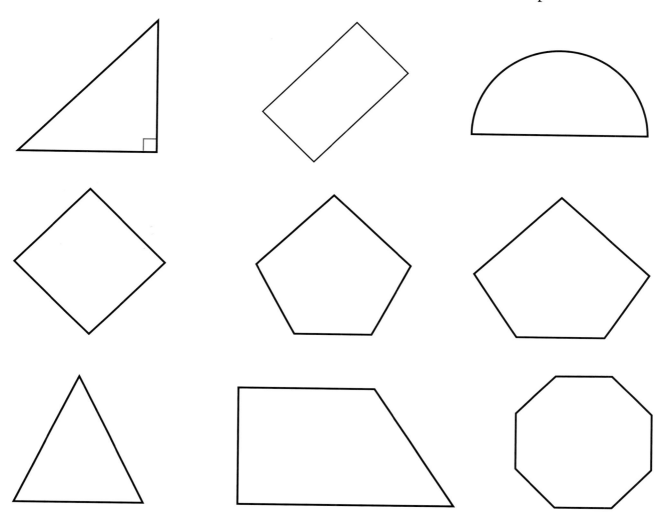

Draw a shape of your own that has only one right angle.

Draw a shape of your own that has no right angles.

This angle is **less than** a right angle.

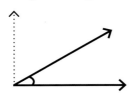

This angle is **more than** a right angle.

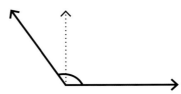

Look at each angle and write "more than," "less than," or "right angle."

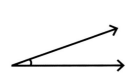

Less than

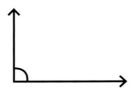

....

....

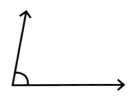

....

....

....

....

....

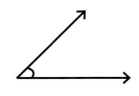

....

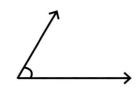

....

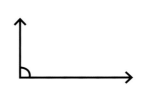

....

Look at the diagram.

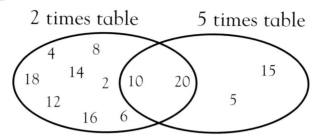

Which numbers are only in the 2 times table?

Which numbers are only in the 5 times table?

Which numbers are in both the 2 and 5 times tables?

Look at the diagram.

	Odd numbers	Even numbers
In 5 times table	15 5	20 10
In 2 times table		4 8 6 18 16 12 10 2 20 14

How many numbers are odd?   How many numbers are even?

Which numbers are even and in the 5 times table?

Why are there no numbers in both the 2 times table and the odd section?

....

Barry's watch shows this time in the evening.

Val's watch shows this time in the evening.

What is the difference between the two times? ....

Sean goes for a long walk and starts at 9:30. The walk takes two and a quarter hours. When does Sean arrive?

The dogs have walked these distances.

14 miles

17 miles

28 miles

How far have the dogs walked in total?

A teacher found out that 24 children had packed lunches, 7 bought school lunch, and 1 went home to lunch.

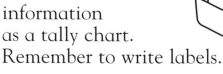

Show this information as a tally chart. Remember to write labels.

Draw a shape that has three sides.

Draw a shape that has two lines of symmetry. Mark the lines of symmetry on your shape.

What is the name of your shape? ....

Check (✔) the angle that is less than a right angle.

Sean divides a number by 3, and the answer is 9. What was the number?

Barbara multiplies a number by 6 and the answer is 66. What was the number?

Which number is 24 more than 24?

Which number is 36 less than 36?

A playground is a rectangle 90 ft by 30 ft.

Darius walks around the sides of the playground. How far does he walk?

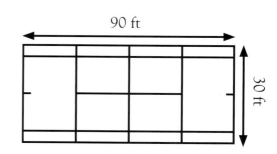

90 ft

30 ft

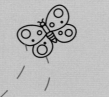

Certificate

Grade 3

Congratulations to

....

for successfully finishing this book.

GOOD JOB!

You're a star.

Date

....

Answer Section
with Parents' Notes

This book is intended to help support children's understanding of mathematics as the processes develop and they become more proficient and fluent in communicating math.

Contents
By working through this book, your child will practice:
- understanding place value of large and negative numbers;
- understanding strategies for multiplying and dividing;
- applying mathematics to solve problems in real-life situations;
- solving problems involving four operations;
- solving money and time problems;
- understanding fractions of objects and numbers;
- recognizing angles;
- using calculators;
- representing and interpreting data;
- reading units of measurement.

How to help your child
Your child should be able to read the more specialized math words ("multiples" for example), but do be prepared to assist. Working with your child also has great benefits in understanding how your child is thinking and where the stumbling blocks may be.

Provide opportunities for practical use of measuring equipment and appropriate tools, such as calculators, rulers, and scales. This will help children to visualize situations.

Build your children's confidence with words of praise. If they are getting answers wrong, encourage them to try again another time.

Good luck, and remember to have fun.

★ Place value

Circle the "tens" digit in each number.

4**5**   12,4**5**8   7,2**0**9   9,5**6**7   7**0**0

Circle the "hundreds" digit in each number.

1**0**84   3**6**5   12,4**5**6   5,**7**86   9,**2**00

Circle the "thousands" digit in each number.

6,000   **2**,163   10,**546**   **5**,284   **9**,534

654 can be written as 600 + 50 + 4. This is called the **expanded form**. Write each number in its expanded form.

423 400 + 20 + 3   9,406 9,000 + 400 + 6

710 700 + 10   8,056 8,000 + 50 + 6

612 600 + 10 + 2   1,428 1,000 + 400 + 20 + 8

649 600 + 40 + 9   10,417 10,000 + 400 + 10 + 7

8,000 + 700 + 60 + 9 can be written as 8,769. This is called the **standard form**. Write each number in its standard form.

2,000 + 400 + 7 2,407   4,000 + 200 + 30 + 5 4,235

6,000 + 50 + 8 6,058   9,000 + 4 9,004

Recognizing the value of a digit is important in many ways and will help children when it comes to using the four arithmetic operations. Being able to "split" numbers as shown in the last two questions can be very helpful.

5

Negative numbers ★

Look at this number line.

-10 -9 -8 -7 -6 -5 -4 -3 -2 -1 0 1 2 3 4 5 6 7 8 9 10

Add 1 to each number. **Note:** When you add, you move to the right on the number line.

3 **4**   7 **8**   9 **10**   1 **2**   0 **1**   -2 **-1**

-10 **-9**   8 **9**   4 **5**   6 **7**   -3 **-2**   -9 **-8**

Subtract 1 from each number. **Note:** When you subtract, you move left on the number line.

8 **7**   5 **4**   10 **9**   1 **0**   -3 **-4**   -9 **-10**

2 **1**   9 **8**   -5 **-6**   4 **3**   -8 **-9**   -7 **-8**

Add 3 to each number. **Hint:** Move to the right.

4 **7**   7 **10**   0 **3**   -7 **-4**   -5 **-2**

5 **8**   -3 **0**   -9 **-6**   6 **9**   -10 **-7**

Subtract 4 from each number. **Hint:** Move to the left.

4 **0**   -5 **-9**   9 **5**   10 **6**   -4 **-8**

5 **1**   2 **-2**   3 **-1**   -1 **-5**   -6 **-10**

At this stage, questions about negative numbers are usually shown with a number line so that children can actually see "where to go" when adding and subtracting.

★ Count forward and backward

What is 3 more than these numbers?

7 **10**   28 **31**   99 **102**   80 **83**   107 **110**

What is 3 less than these numbers?

11 **8**   70 **67**   92 **89**   48 **45**   101 **98**

What is 4 more than these numbers?

6 **10**   17 **21**   59 **63**   31 **35**   98 **102**

What is 4 less than these numbers?

11 **7**   34 **30**   43 **39**   98 **94**   102 **98**

Fill in the missing numbers.

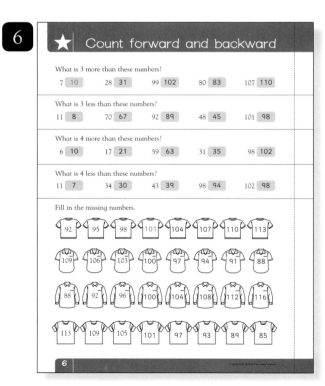

92 95 **98** 101 104 **107** 110 **113**

109 106 **103** 100 **97** 94 **91** 88

88 92 96 **100** 104 **108** 112 **116**

113 **109** 105 101 **97** 93 **89** 85

This work should be straightforward. Encourage children to solve the simple problems quickly and without using fingers. Children may have a slight problem when crossing into the 100s if they are unsure about place values.

7

Ordering numbers ★

Put each row of numbers in order, starting with the smallest.

213   312   123   230   32
32   **123**   **213**   **230**   **312**

841   148   184   481   814
148   **184**   **481**   **814**   **841**

Put each row of numbers in order, starting with the largest.

672   276   627   267   726
726   **672**   **627**   **276**   **267**

1,500   1,005   1,050   5,000   5,100
5,100   **5,000**   **1,500**   **1,050**   **1,005**

Put this row in order, starting with the smallest amount.

$2.60 $6.20 $2.06 $6.02 $0.26
$0.26   **$2.06**   **$2.60**   **$6.02**   **$6.20**

Put this row in order, starting with the largest amount.

$12.34 $21.43 $43.21 $43.12 $34.21
$43.21   **$43.12**   **$34.21**   **$21.43**   **$12.34**

For each sum, put these numbers in order, starting with the largest. Then add.

50 + 200 + 8 = **200** + **50** + **8** = **258**

7 + 60 + 400 = **400** + **60** + **7** = **467**

12 + 750 = **750** + **12** = **762**

24 + 370 = **370** + **24** = **394**

Children will generally be able to arrange smaller numbers but can become confused with higher numbers. Help them by looking at the first digit first, ex. the 2 of 276, and arranging the hundreds, and then the tens, and then the ones.

★ Rounding

Round each number to the nearest 10.

14 **10**   9 **10**   55 **60**   26 **30**

11 **10**   38 **40**   99 **100**   72 **70**

883 **880**   451 **450**   724 **720**   906 **910**

107 **110**   2,345 **2,350**   4,189 **4,190**   6,503 **6,500**

Round each number to the nearest 100.

263 **300**   485 **500**   210 **200**   895 **900**

481 **500**   673 **700**   950 **1,000**   420 **400**

762 **800**   380 **400**   266 **300**   750 **800**

Round each number to the nearest 1,000.

1,070 **1,000**   1,430 **1,000**   3,760 **4,000**   2,888 **3,000**

4,500 **5,000**   6,731 **7,000**   9,244 **9,000**   6,499 **6,000**

8,050 **8,000**   6,370 **6,000**   7,500 **8,000**   9,482 **9,000**

8

As with all rounding, it is the "5," "50," or "500" situation that can cause confusion. The simple convention is to round upwards so that 15 will become 20, for example.

Comparing numbers ★

Circle the smaller number.

(3 x 4) or 7 + 6   (7 + 8) or 20 – 4   2 x 8 or (3 x 5)

(10 x 3) or 18 + 13   5 x 4 or (10 + 9)   (15 – 3) or 8 + 6

Circle the larger number.

(10 x 4) or 19 + 13   8 + 9 or (3 x 6)   (12 + 12) or 7 x 3

(5 x 3) or 8 + 6   10 + 12 or (5 x 5)   7 + 13 or (30 – 9)

Circle the smaller amount.

$2.00 or (80 ¢ + 70 ¢)   65 ¢ – 25 ¢ or (56 ¢ – 30 ¢)

($1.00) or 70 ¢ + 35 ¢   90 ¢ – 25 ¢ or (65 ¢ – 10 ¢)

Circle the larger amount.

($5 + $2) or 250 ¢ + 250 ¢   (47 ¢ – 8 ¢) or 35 ¢ + 3¢

$2.50 or ($3.00 – 40 ¢)   60 ¢ – 15 ¢ or (70 ¢ – 20 ¢)

Circle the amount that is between $3.00 and $4.00.

$2.30 + 65 ¢   ($5.00 – $1.50) $5.00 – 35 ¢

Circle the amount that is between 2 ft and 3 ft.

1.5 ft + 2.5 ft   6.5 ft – 2.5 ft   (4 ft – 1.5 ft)

9

This is practice in working out answers and then comparing the results. Children should learn to read questions carefully, as with this selection they are asked to both "circle the larger number" and "circle the smaller number."

★ Fractions of numbers

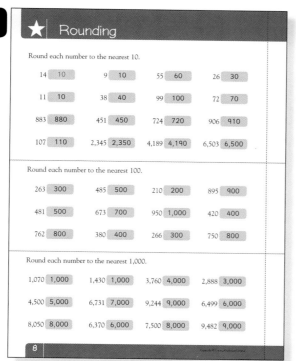

Circle half ($\frac{1}{2}$) of the vegetables in each group.

Circle a quarter ($\frac{1}{4}$) of the fruit in each row.

What is half ($\frac{1}{2}$) of each number?

6 **3**   12 **6**   10 **5**   20 **10**   4 **2**

What is a quarter ($\frac{1}{4}$) of each number?

4 **1**   8 **2**   16 **4**   20 **5**   12 **3**

Half of a number is 3. What is the number?   **6**

Half of a number is 6. What is the number?   **12**

A quarter of a number is 1. What is the number?   **4**

A quarter of a number is 5. What is the number?   **20**

10

Once children have counted the number of each item, they should be able to work out a half or quarter fairly quickly. Where images are not given, and children are struggling, encourage them to draw circles to then split up equally.

Fractions of shapes ★

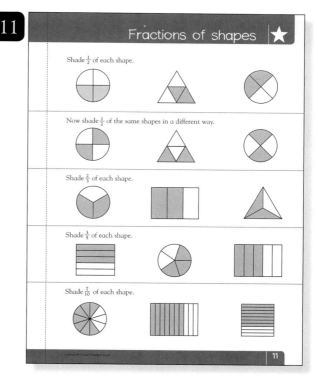

Shade $\frac{1}{4}$ of each shape.

Now shade $\frac{1}{4}$ of the same shapes in a different way.

Shade $\frac{2}{3}$ of each shape.

Shade $\frac{3}{5}$ of each shape.

Shade $\frac{7}{10}$ of each shape.

11

Children should realize that the actual sections that are shaded do not matter as long as the correct number are shaded.

★ Quarters

What is a quarter ($\frac{1}{4}$) of each number?

12 **3**　　16 **4**　　40 **10**　　28 **7**

What is a quarter ($\frac{1}{4}$) of each amount?

4 ¢ **1 ¢**　　20 ¢ **5 ¢**　　12 ¢ **3 ¢**　　16 ¢ **4 ¢**

How much is a quarter ($\frac{1}{4}$) of 40 ¢?

10 ¢

Fido eats 8 biscuits each day. Fido has a quarter ($\frac{1}{4}$) of the biscuits for breakfast. How many biscuits does Fido have for breakfast?　　**2**

Daisy is given 20 CDs by her sister. Daisy gives a quarter ($\frac{1}{4}$) of the CDs to her brother. How many CDs does Daisy give to her brother?

5

Shen has to work for one hour but stops after a quarter ($\frac{1}{4}$) of an hour. How long is a quarter of an hour in minutes?　　**15 minutes**

Darius has to wait 24 minutes for a bus. He has waited a quarter ($\frac{1}{4}$) of that time. How long does Darius still have to wait?

18 minutes

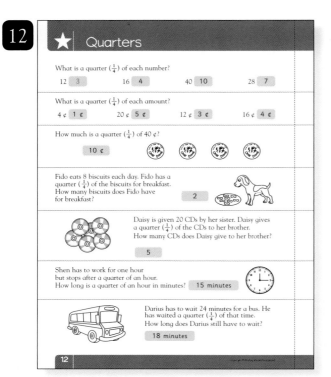

Children generally find quarters a little trickier than halves, so the more practice, the better. They need to be careful answering the last question, which is deliberately a bit more complicated.

13

Calculator ★

Use a calculator to work out these problems.

7 x 12 = **84**	9 x 9 = **81**	10 x 12 = **120**
7 x 6 = **42**	14 x 10 = **140**	12 x 50 = **600**
16 x 3 = **48**	200 x 6 = **1,200**	120 x 7 = **840**
12 x 8 = **96**	20 x 20 = **400**	150 x 6 = **900**
26 + 49 + 58 = **133**	74 + 59 + 82 = **215**	29 + 69 + 84 = **182**
546 + 512 = **1,058**	785 + 897 = **1,682**	209 + 109 + 56 = **374**
432 + 777 = **1,209**	812 + 564 = **1,376**	231 + 321 + 412 = **964**
576 − 299 = **277**	600 − 345 = **255**	708 − 544 = **164**
1,000 − 564 = **436**	1,645 − 789 = **856**	1,705 − 805 = **900**
5,634 − 4,867 = **767**	4,554 − 3,667 = **887**	9,045 − 9,044 = **1**
86 ÷ 2 = **43**	100 ÷ 25 = **4**	40 ÷ 8 = **5**
160 ÷ 8 = **20**	240 ÷ 12 = **20**	300 ÷ 15 = **20**
4,800 ÷ 200 = **24**	5,000 ÷ 25 = **200**	196 ÷ 14 = **14**

Jake has to share $280 equally between himself and his four sisters.

How much will they each receive?　　**$56**

Children usually pick up calculator skills very quickly and enjoy using them. Encourage them to make estimates of answers before pressing the keys. Estimates can be done by rounding the numbers, a skill that should already have been learned.

14

★ Keeping skills sharp

Which child has the most money?

Nada　Barbara　Ann　Harris
$2,304　$432　$4,023　$3,402　　**Ann**

This thermometer shows the temperature. Overnight, the temperature drops by 14°. What is the temperature at night?

−2°F

Write the children's names in order of height, starting with the shortest.

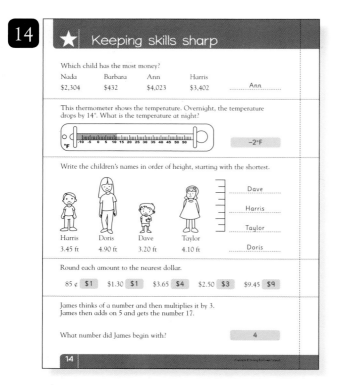

Harris　Doris　Dave　Taylor
3.45 ft　4.90 ft　3.20 ft　4.10 ft

Dave
Harris
Taylor
Doris

Round each amount to the nearest dollar.

85 ¢ **$1**　　$1.30 **$1**　　$3.65 **$4**　　$2.50 **$3**　　$9.45 **$9**

James thinks of a number and then multiplies it by 3. James then adds on 5 and gets the number 17.

What number did James begin with?　　**4**

The questions on pages 14 and 15 review the work on the preceding pages and can also be used as a test.

15

Keeping skills sharp ★

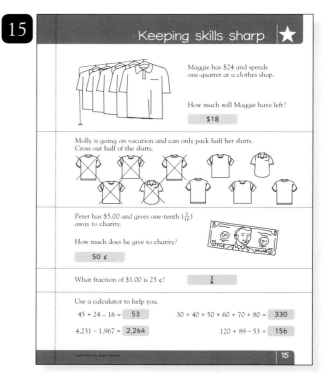

Maggie has $24 and spends one-quarter at a clothes shop.

How much will Maggie have left?　　**$18**

Molly is going on vacation and can only pack half her shirts. Cross out half of the shirts.

Peter has $5.00 and gives one-tenth ($\frac{1}{10}$) away to charity.

How much does he give to charity?　　**50 ¢**

What fraction of $1.00 is 25 ¢?　　**$\frac{1}{4}$**

Use a calculator to help you.

45 + 24 − 16 = **53**　　30 + 40 + 50 + 60 + 70 + 80 = **330**

4,231 − 1,967 = **2,264**　　120 + 89 − 53 = **156**

★ Adding three numbers

Write the answers.

9 + 8 + 7 = 24   10 + 8 + 7 = 25   20 + 17 + 14 = 51

11 + 5 + 3 = 19   15 + 10 + 5 = 30   30 + 20 + 10 = 60

50 + 30 + 10 = 90   12 + 11 + 10 = 33   21 + 11 + 1 = 33

7 + 14 + 21 = 42   9 + 18 + 30 = 57   50 + 30 + 20 = 100

40 + 18 + 20 = 78   30 + 19 + 10 = 59   10 + 23 + 40 = 73

70 + 9 + 10 = 89   50 + 17 + 20 = 87   40 + 20 + 40 = 100

17 + 18 + 19 = 54   23 + 24 + 25 = 72   36 + 37 + 38 = 111

51 + 52 + 53 = 156   35 + 45 + 55 = 135   20 + 80 + 60 = 160

Write the answers.

23	45	19	56	38	73
34	16	15	42	13	12
+ 42	+ 18	+ 32	+ 17	+ 25	+ 15
99	79	66	115	76	100

Generally it is good to have children rearrange
the numbers in descending order before adding.
Column addition is often taught at this age and
appears more formal than the sums laid out in
rows. The key is to "carry" a number from the
ones to the tens if it totals more than 9.

Subtracting ★

Write the answers.

20 − 7 = 13   34 − 18 = 16   42 − 19 = 23   23 − 22 = 1

50 − 27 = 23   44 − 35 = 9   21 − 19 = 2   50 − 36 = 14

53 − 26 = 27   71 − 68 = 3   49 − 17 = 32   60 − 12 = 48

50 − 19 = 31   40 − 18 = 22   30 − 17 = 13   20 − 16 = 4

100 − 40 = 60   100 − 65 = 35   100 − 32 = 68   100 − 17 = 83

100 − 45 = 55   100 − 70 = 30   100 − 23 = 77   100 − 71 = 29

Write the answers.

43	67	80	120	105	102
− 21	− 14	− 54	− 30	− 45	− 56
22	53	26	90	60	46

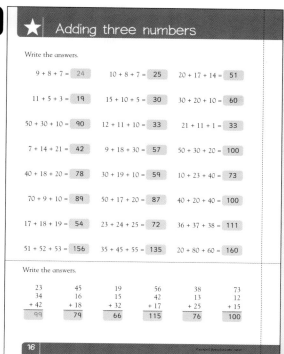

Matilda owns 145 pairs of shoes but
gives 62 pairs away to a charity shop.

How many pairs of shoes does
Matilda have left?

83

Schools will teach different ways of solving
subtraction questions and children may easily
become confused, so take everything very slowly.
A common method is to "add upwards." For
14 − 8, go up from 8 to 10 = +2, then go up
from 10 to 14 = +4. Finish by adding: 2 + 4 = 6.

★ Groups of 2

Write the answers.

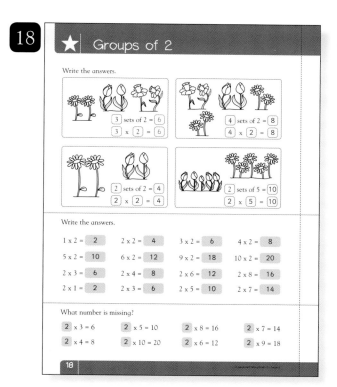

3 sets of 2 = 6
3 x 2 = 6

4 sets of 2 = 8
4 x 2 = 8

2 sets of 2 = 4
2 x 2 = 4

2 sets of 5 = 10
2 x 5 = 10

Write the answers.

1 x 2 = 2   2 x 2 = 4   3 x 2 = 6   4 x 2 = 8

5 x 2 = 10   6 x 2 = 12   9 x 2 = 18   10 x 2 = 20

2 x 3 = 6   2 x 4 = 8   2 x 6 = 12   2 x 8 = 16

2 x 1 = 2   2 x 3 = 6   2 x 5 = 10   2 x 7 = 14

What number is missing?

2 x 3 = 6   2 x 5 = 10   2 x 8 = 16   2 x 7 = 14

2 x 4 = 8   2 x 10 = 20 2 x 6 = 12   2 x 9 = 18

This page provides the starting point for
multiplication. At this stage, the more formal
questions will usually be laid out horizontally
rather than vertically.

2x table ★

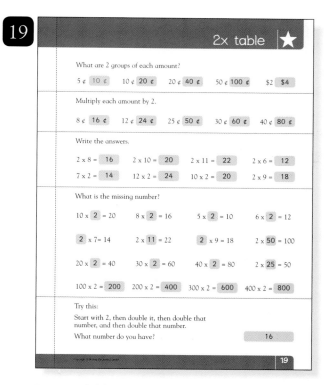

What are 2 groups of each amount?

5 ¢ 10 ¢   10 ¢ 20 ¢   20 ¢ 40 ¢   50 ¢ 100 ¢ $2 $4

Multiply each amount by 2.

8 ¢ 16 ¢   12 ¢ 24 ¢   25 ¢ 50 ¢   30 ¢ 60 ¢   40 ¢ 80 ¢

Write the answers.

2 x 8 = 16   2 x 10 = 20   2 x 11 = 22   2 x 6 = 12

7 x 2 = 14   12 x 2 = 24   10 x 2 = 20   2 x 9 = 18

What is the missing number?

10 x 2 = 20   8 x 2 = 16   5 x 2 = 10   6 x 2 = 12

2 x 7 = 14   2 x 11 = 22   2 x 9 = 18   2 x 50 = 100

20 x 2 = 40   30 x 2 = 60   40 x 2 = 80   2 x 25 = 50

100 x 2 = 200   200 x 2 = 400   300 x 2 = 600   400 x 2 = 800

Try this:

Start with 2, then double it, then double that
number, and then double that number.

What number do you have?   16

By now children should have a good knowledge
of the 2 times tables, and this page provides more
practice. Look out for two things: the children's
accurate recall of the tables, and fast recall.

★ 10x table

Match each dog to the right bone with a line.

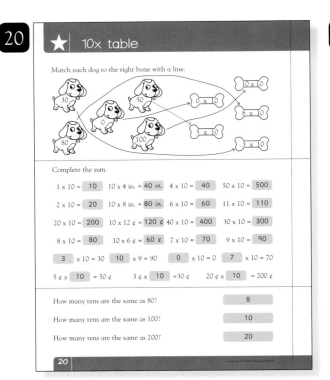

Complete the sum.

1 x 10 = 10   10 x 4 in. = 40 in.   4 x 10 = 40   50 x 10 = 500

2 x 10 = 20   10 x 8 in. = 80 in.   6 x 10 = 60   11 x 10 = 110

20 x 10 = 200   10 x 12 ¢ = 120 ¢   40 x 10 = 400   30 x 10 = 300

8 x 10 = 80   10 x 6 ¢ = 60 ¢   7 x 10 = 70   9 x 10 = 90

3 x 10 = 30   10 x 9 = 90   0 x 10 = 0   7 x 10 = 70

5 ¢ x 10 = 50 ¢   3 ¢ x 10 = 30 ¢   20 ¢ x 10 = 200 ¢

How many tens are the same as 80?   8

How many tens are the same as 100?   10

How many tens are the same as 200?   20

20

Children will be gaining confidence with the 10 times table as well. Keep a record of how quickly and accurately they complete this page. Encourage them to try it again on another occasion if further practice is needed.

5x table ★

Match each mouse to the right cheese with a line.

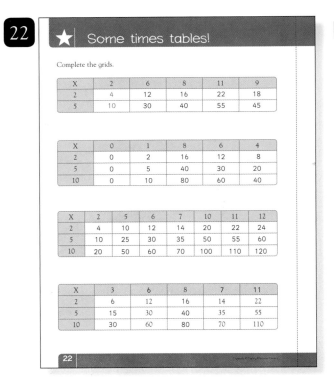

Write the answers.

4 x 5 = 20   8 x 5 = 40   5 x 3 ¢ = 15 ¢   5 x 0 = 0

1 x 5 = 5   11 x 5 = 55   5 x 9 ¢ = 45 ¢   5 x 12 ¢ = 60 ¢

6 x 5 = 30   7 x 5 = 35   5 x 10 in. = 50 in.   5 x 6 = 30

12 x 5 = 60   0 x 5 = 0   5 x 6 ¢ = 30 ¢   5 x 9 = 45

Circle the numbers that are **not** multiples of 5.

5   10   ⑬   40   90   55   120   ⑱   ㉒   ㊼   100

Write the answers.

5 + 5 = 10   2 groups of 5 = 10   5 groups of 2 are 10

5 x 2 = 10   3 groups of 5 = 15   3 groups of 5 are 15

21

This 5 times table practice also reinforces the different ways of presenting multiplication problems and the terminology used.

★ Some times tables!

Complete the grids.

X	2	6	8	11	9
2	4	12	16	22	18
5	10	30	40	55	45

X	0	1	8	6	4
2	0	2	16	12	8
5	0	5	40	30	20
10	0	10	80	60	40

X	2	5	6	7	10	11	12
2	4	10	12	14	20	22	24
5	10	25	30	35	50	55	60
10	20	50	60	70	100	110	120

X	3	6	8	7	11
2	6	12	16	14	22
5	15	30	40	35	55
10	30	60	80	70	110

22

These grids test knowledge of the 2, 5, and 10 times tables. As before, it is not just accurate recall but very quick recall that needs to be achieved.

Multiplying ★

Write the answers.

9 x 3 = 27   10 x 6 = 60   8 x 4 = 32   6 x 11 = 66

7 x 5 = 35   9 x 4 = 36   6 x 5 = 30   10 x 10 = 100

12 x 2 = 24   12 x 4 = 48   12 x 10 = 120   12 x 0 = 0

4 x 7 = 28   5 x 9 = 45   3 x 8 = 24   7 x 10 = 70

1 x 1 = 1   3 x 3 = 9   5 x 5 = 25   6 x 6 = 36

7 x 7 = 49   8 x 8 = 64   9 x 9 = 81   0 x 0 = 0

Write the answers.

```
  8          7          9         10
x 4        x 6        x 5        x 8
 32         42         45         80

 12         13         14         15
x 7        x 4        x 6        x 8
 84         52         84        120
```

Don collects 12 new sports cards every day for a week.

How many cards will Don have at the end of the week?

84

23

These multiplication questions may appear to have times tables that have not been covered yet, such as 9 x 5. It is important that children realize that the answer is the same as 5 x 9, which they should know already.

★ Multiples

Circle the numbers that are multiples of 3.

(12) 14 16 (18) 20 22 (24) 26 28 (30)

Circle the numbers that are multiples of 4.

2 (4) 6 (8) 10 (12) 14 (16) 18 (20)

Circle the numbers that are multiples of 5.

2 7 (10) 14 19 (20) (25) 28 33 42

Circle the numbers that are multiples of 6.

4 (6) 8 10 (12) 14 16 (18) 20 (24)

Circle the numbers that are multiples of 10.

5 (10) (20) (30) 55 75 (90) 95 (100) (200)

What is the smallest number that is a multiple of 3 and 4?	12
What is the smallest number that is a multiple of 2 and 5?	10
What is the smallest number that is a multiple of 3 and 5?	15
What is the smallest number that is a multiple of 2 and 4?	4
What is the smallest number that is a multiple of 3 and 10?	30

Children will associate multiples with "numbers in the times tables." The last five questions are a little more challenging but will test understanding.

Dividing ★

Write the answers.

20 ÷ 4 = 5	20 ÷ 2 = 10	20 ÷ 5 = 4
20 ÷ 10 = 2	12 ÷ 2 = 6	12 ÷ 6 = 2
12 ÷ 3 = 4	12 ÷ 4 = 3	18 ÷ 3 = 6
18 ÷ 6 = 3	18 ÷ 9 = 2	18 ÷ 2 = 9
30 ÷ 6 = 5	24 ÷ 2 = 12	40 ÷ 10 = 4
28 ÷ 7 = 4	44 ÷ 4 = 11	25 ÷ 5 = 5
32 ÷ 8 = 4	24 ÷ 6 = 4	12 ÷ 12 = 1
14 ÷ 2 = 7	32 ÷ 4 = 8	56 ÷ 7 = 8
10 ÷ 5 = 2	14 ÷ 2 = 7	20 ÷ 4 = 5
24 ÷ 3 = 8	12 ÷ 2 = 6	15 ÷ 5 = 3
21 ÷ 3 = 7	27 ÷ 3 = 9	16 ÷ 4 = 4
36 ÷ 4 = 9	28 ÷ 4 = 7	30 ÷ 5 = 6
50 ÷ 10 = 5	70 ÷ 10 = 7	60 ÷ 10 = 6
40 ÷ 10 = 4	16 ÷ 2 = 8	22 ÷ 2 = 11
4 ÷ 2 = 2	14 ÷ 2 = 7	24 ÷ 3 = 8
45 ÷ 5 = 9	44 ÷ 4 = 11	12 ÷ 6 = 2

It is most important that children realize the connection between simple division and times tables.

★ Choosing the operation

I add 16 to a number and then have 40. What number did I begin with?	24
I subtract 25 from a number and have 14 left. What number did I start with?	39
I multiplied a number by 6 and now have 54. What number did I begin with?	9
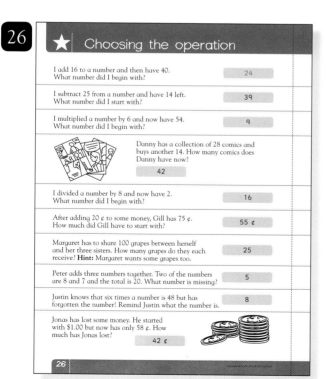 Danny has a collection of 28 comics and buys another 14. How many comics does Danny have now?	42
I divided a number by 8 and now have 2. What number did I begin with?	16
After adding 20 ¢ to some money, Gill has 75 ¢. How much did Gill have to start with?	55 ¢
Margaret has to share 100 grapes between herself and her three sisters. How many grapes do they each receive? **Hint:** Margaret wants some grapes too.	25
Peter adds three numbers together. Two of the numbers are 8 and 7 and the total is 20. What number is missing?	5
Justin knows that six times a number is 48 but has forgotten the number! Remind Justin what the number is.	8
Jonas has lost some money. He started with $1.00 but now has only 58 ¢. How much has Jonas lost?	42 ¢

The practical application of the four operations is very important, but children usually have few opportunities to do this. It is essential to know that subtraction is the reverse of addition, and that division is the reverse of multiplication.

Working with money ★

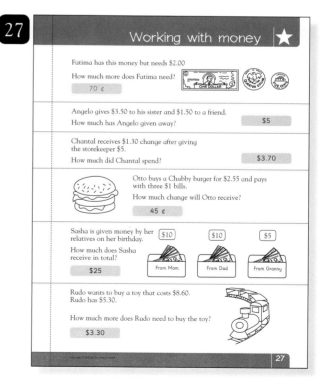

Fatima has this money but needs $2.00 How much more does Fatima need?	70 ¢
Angelo gives $3.50 to his sister and $1.50 to a friend. How much has Angelo given away?	$5
Chantal receives $1.30 change after giving the storekeeper $5. How much did Chantal spend?	$3.70
Otto buys a Chubby burger for $2.55 and pays with three $1 bills. How much change will Otto receive?	45 ¢
Sasha is given money by her relatives on her birthday. $10 $10 $5 How much does Sasha receive in total? From Mom From Dad From Granny	$25
Rudo wants to buy a toy that costs $8.60. Rudo has $5.30. How much more does Rudo need to buy the toy?	$3.30

Have some coins and bills available to help children if necessary.

★ Money problems

When Henry's dad empties his pockets, he finds he has one $10 bill, two $5 bills, four 25 ¢ coins, and five 10 ¢ coins.

How much money has Henry's dad found? $21.50

Henry's mom finds this money behind some cushions—four $1 bills, five 25 ¢ coins, two 10 ¢ coins, and seven 1 ¢ coins.

How much money has Henry's mom found? $5.52

Henry's mom and dad put their money together.
How much do they have in total?
$27.02

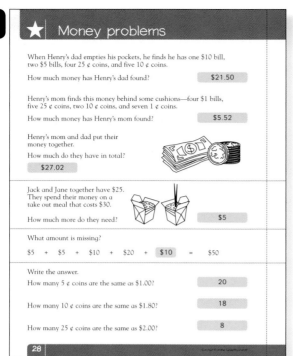

Jack and Jane together have $25.
They spend their money on a take out meal that costs $30.

How much more do they need? $5

What amount is missing?

$5 + $5 + $10 + $20 + **$10** = $50

Write the answer.

How many 5 ¢ coins are the same as $1.00?   20

How many 10 ¢ coins are the same as $1.80?   18

How many 25 ¢ coins are the same as $2.00?   8

The last question helps to check that children know how many 5¢, 10 ¢, and 25¢ coins are needed to make up $1.00. They can use this information to calculate the number for other amounts too.

Decimals with money ★

Write each amount in two ways.

Example: Thirty-five cents is either 35 ¢ or $0.35

Seven cents	7 ¢	$0.07	Ninety cents	90 ¢	$0.90
Twenty-nine cents	29 ¢	$0.29	Forty-two cents	42 ¢	$0.42
Thirty-one cents	31 ¢	$0.31	Fifteen cents	15 ¢	$0.15
Sixty-seven cents	67 ¢	$0.67	Fifty-five cents	55 ¢	$0.55
Ninety-three cents	93 ¢	$0.93	Seventy-eight cents	78 ¢	$0.78

Write the answers.

$1.20 + $0.80 = **$2** $1.30 + $1.60 = **$2.90** $2.10 + $1.70 = **$3.80**

$1.30 + $0.50 = **$1.80** $5.00 − $2.50 = **$2.50** $1.45 + $0.65 = **$2.10**

$2.50 + $1.50 = **$4.00** $1.40 + $2.30 = **$3.70** $5.25 + $1.15 = **$6.40**

$1.35 + $1.45 = **$2.80** $0.60 + $0.85 = **$1.45** $1.60 + $1.60 = **$3.20**

$4.45 + $0.70 = **$5.15** $2.05 + $1.75 = **$3.80** $1.00 − $0.73 = **$0.27**

$1.00 − $0.30 = **$0.70** $5.90 + $0.20 = **$6.10** $2.00 − $1.50 = **$0.50**

$2.00 − $0.50 = **$1.50** $5.00 − $3.00 = **$2.00** $10.00 − $7.50 = **$2.50**

Write the answers.

What is $1.60 plus 45 ¢? **$2.05**   How much is $5.00 minus 8 ¢? **$4.92**

What is $3.80 plus 70 ¢? **$4.50**   How much is $2.00 minus 30 ¢? **$1.70**

Children should understand the conventions we use for writing money, ex. $3.45, $0.24, or 24 ¢. It is correct to write an amount as 537 ¢, for example, but this is very seldom done.

★ Keeping skills sharp

Complete this grid.

X	4	9	10	6
5	20	45	50	30
2	8	18	20	12

Write the answers.

```
  24        38        40        51
- 17      - 12      - 23      - 36
   7        26        17        15
```

Bart has to mark these products for Homer.
Help Bart to mark the products right (✔) or wrong (✘).

8 x 3 = 42 **✘**   5 x 6 = 30 **✔**   2 x 12 = 22 **✘**

10 x 5 = 50 **✔**   3 x 9 = 24 **✘**   8 x 4 = 31 **✘**

What is the smallest number that is a multiple of 4 and 5?   20

What is the largest number that is a multiple of 3 and 2 but less than 20?   18

Lucy has to share 3 pizzas equally between herself and three friends. Each pizza has 8 pieces.

How many pieces of pizza will each girl receive?   6

The test on this page and the following one cover work in the previous pages. It may be worth timing children to see how quickly they can work through the questions, but do not put pressure on them unnecessarily.

Keeping skills sharp ★

Share 20 apples equally among 4 children.

How many apples will each child get?
5

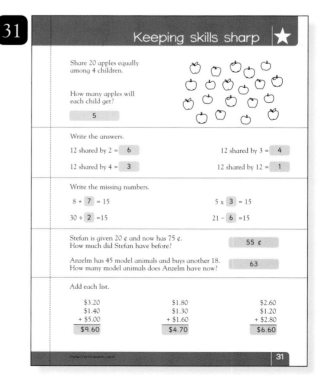

Write the answers.

12 shared by 2 = **6**   12 shared by 3 = **4**

12 shared by 4 = **3**   12 shared by 12 = **1**

Write the missing numbers.

8 + **7** = 15   5 x **3** = 15

30 ÷ **2** =15   21 − **6** =15

Stefan is given 20 ¢ and now has 75 ¢.
How much did Stefan have before?   55 ¢

Anzelm has 45 model animals and buys another 18.
How many model animals does Anzelm have now?   63

Add each list.

```
  $3.20         $1.80         $2.60
  $1.40         $1.30         $1.20
+ $5.00       + $1.60       + $2.80
  $9.60         $4.70         $6.60
```